THE INUIT
HUNTERS OF THE NORTH

Dedication

Atuagaq una Itukusuk Kristiansen-mut
aamaa Hans Jensen-mut Pigitipara.

This book is for Itukusuk Kristiansen
and Hans Jensen.

Each of the Arctic's Inuit communities has developed its own yearly cycle of life, each varying, sometimes considerably, from one area of the Arctic to another. This book focuses on the traditional life of one particular Inuit group known as the 'Polar Eskimos' of Northwest Greenland. It does so for no other reason than that this is the group with which we have spent the most time.

The Authors

CLB 1973

Printed and bound in Barcelona, Spain by Cronion, S.A.
Colour separations by Hong Kong Graphic Arts Ltd, Hong Kong.
ISBN 0 86283 612 3

DEP. LEG. B-31.675-88

THE INUIT
HUNTERS OF THE NORTH

Text and Photography by
Bryan and Cherry Alexander

Bramley Books

The land of the Inuit is vast. Spanning two continents, it covers the northern regions of the Soviet Union, Alaska, Canada and Greenland. It's a land that is visited by comparatively few outsiders, and for many who live in lower latitudes it has the image of a wild and forbidding icy wilderness. 'Up here on Baffin Island', a Hudson Bay Company worker once joked to me, 'We have ten months winter and two months bad snowmobiling'. As with many similar jokes, there is an element of truth in it. Most of the Inuit homeland does lie within the Arctic circle and, yes, it is cold up there, but the low winter temperatures are no more severe than those experienced by some central areas of North America like Minnesota or Manitoba. What makes the Arctic different is that there is little relief, the freezing temperatures persisting for much of the year.

Despite this, the Arctic is a place of often breathtaking beauty, with magnificent mountains, plains, fjords and glaciers that produce spectacular icebergs. It is also remarkably rich in wildlife and is home for the polar bear, and other animals such as the walrus, caribou, musk-ox, and seal. In the brief summer much of the land is covered with a blanket of brightly-coloured flowers, and millions of sea birds arrive to raise their young, exploiting the prolific food chain of the plankton-rich polar seas. The Arctic may be few people's idea of paradise, but for the Inuit it is home; a beautiful land and one which until comparatively recently could provide them with everything they could possibly need.

The first ancestors of today's Inuit are believed to have been an Arctic Mongol people who migrated from Siberia between twelve and fifteen thousand years ago. The last Ice Age, 30-15,000 B.C., froze a vast mass of water resulting in a considerable drop in the sea level. That in turn created a land bridge across the Bering Strait, which separates Alaska from Siberia. These early hunters followed the herds of caribou and musk-oxen across the land bridge before settling on the Arctic shores of Alaska. It seems likely that these migrations continued to some extent even after the land bridge was once again engulfed by the sea, for the Bering Strait is under sixty miles wide, not an impossible journey in an *umiak* (skin boat), and the two Diomede Islands mid-way would have provided a convenient stopover.

Around 3,000 B.C. these Inuit forbears began to spread out in search of new hunting areas, migrating eastwards across northern Canada before finally reaching Greenland around 2,000 B.C. Comparatively little is known about these people or what brought about the demise of their culture around 800 B.C., but it is assumed that the unconquerable nature of the Arctic was eventually to prove too much for them.

About the same time, another Arctic culture emerged, known now as the Dorset culture. It is thought to have originated in the northern Hudson Bay area and to have spread across a vast area of Canada and Greenland. The Dorset people were mainly inland caribou hunters, though they are known to have hunted sea mammals as well, but not the great whales. For although they had umiaks they lacked the necessary skill to use them for hunting. They had sleds but no dogs, so they had to manhaul them across the tundra. They used harpoons but had no knowledge of the bow and arrow. Their homes were turf houses where they burnt blubber for both light and heat, using pots of hollowed out soapstone to cook in. Perhaps surprisingly, they proved to be remarkably fine artists, carving small figures of men and animals, mainly in bone and ivory. For almost two thousand years the Dorset people were to remain the lords of the Arctic. Their demise was brought about by the emergence of another culture from the Bering sea area around 900 A.D. known as the Thule culture.

The Thule Inuit were a coastal people, extremely skilled hunters, and much better equipped for surviving in the Arctic than their predecessors. They had dogs to pull their sledges in winter and kayaks to hunt from in the summer. They also had umiaks, from which they hunted the bowhead whale. Their hunting techniques were much more refined than that of the earlier Inuit. They used the bow and arrow, harpoons, lances, leisters (pronged fish spears) and had a wide variety of other hunting equipment and tools. With all these resources available it is not altogether surprising that the Thule culture flourished. Within 300 years it had spread across the Arctic from Alaska to Greenland, absorbing or destroying the Dorset culture en route. It is from these Thule people that today's Inuit are directly descended.

The Inuits' first experience of white men was with the early arctic explorers searching for the Northwest Passage and other elusive geographical goals. The explorers were quick to realise the importance of using the Inuit on their expeditions. Unlike white men, the Inuit were in their element and understood the ever-changing ways of the Arctic's ice and weather. They usually knew where to find game and their skill at hunting made them invaluable suppliers of fresh meat. And, after the mistakes were made, the ships crushed by the ice and the men left stranded at the mercy of the elements, it was the knowledge, experience and unselfishness of the Inuit that enabled many an Arctic explorer to live to tell the tale.

By the mid-nineteenth century the Inuit began to have regular contact with whalers. The presence of the whaling fleets in the Arctic was to have disastrous consequences for the Inuit. The whalers almost annihilated the bowhead whale, which the Inuit had long depended on, and they brought diseases from the south that the Inuit had little or no resistance to. Sickness spread through the hunting camps, decimating the population and wiping out some communities altogether. But the most far-reaching consequence was that by now the Inuit were already dependent on the white man for the knives, wood, guns and ammunition he could supply. The land they inhabited no longer provided all they required to live.

The whalers were followed into the Arctic by traders eager for the furs that the Inuit could provide, for these were the pioneering days of the famous Hudson Bay Company. Inevitably, missionaries were next to arrive on the scene, with the administrators not far behind them. Settlements were established and the Inuit were 'encouraged', and sometimes forced, to abandon their traditional, semi-nomadic life in hunting camps for a more sedentary existence in villages with modern housing, schools and medical facilities.

There are a little over 100,000 Inuit in the world today – around 1,500 in Siberia, 25,000 in Canada, 30,000 in Alaska and 43,000 in Greenland. Mostly they live in small groups of isolated settlements that are scattered right across the Arctic. Their homes are likely to be small, single storey wooden houses. They don't live in igloos – in fact, only the Inuit from the central Canadian Arctic ever did. For the rest the igloo was never more than a temporary hunting shelter. In former times their homes were sod houses cut into the ground with a roof supported by whalebones and driftwood. A snow house, which in English we refer to as an igloo, the Inuit call *igdluigaq*. Igloo to them simply means a 'house' of any material, shape or size.

The Inuit speak two main languages, though there are numerous local dialects. The Inuit of Siberia and southwest Alaska speak *Yupik*, while the rest of the Inuit right the way across to Greenland speak *Inupiaq*, or *Inuktitut* as it is more commonly known. They call themselves *Inuit* which means 'people' and prefer it to *Eskimo* a name given to them by outsiders and derived from an Algonquian Indian word meaning 'He eats it raw.'

The Polar Eskimos of Northwest Greenland live further north than any other Inuit group. Theirs is the most northerly native community in the world, some 800 miles from the North Pole in the Thule district of Greenland, about as isolated a place as you can find on this earth. Until their discovery in 1816 by the British explorer John Ross, their isolation had led them to believe that they were the only people on earth.

It was the U.S. explorer Robert Peary who first focused world attention on the Polar Eskimos by using them on expeditions in his repeated attempts to reach the North Pole. They were to prove invaluable to him during their twenty-year association. The Inuit respected Peary and one can only presume that it was mainly out of this respect, helped no doubt by the guns, knives and other useful things he gave them, that they regularly and willingly risked their lives for him. It must have been impossible for them to comprehend his motives for wanting to reach the North Pole. For although the Inuit like to travel and hunt in new places, the idea of travelling just to reach a geographical point was totally alien to them. For the Polar Eskimos the North Pole held no attraction; there were no animals to hunt and consequently no food. Their experiences with Peary up there led them to give it the nickname *Kingmersoriartorfigssuak* (the place where one must eat dogs). Today, the older people still refer to the North Pole by this name. To the young however, *kingmersoriartorfigssuak* means something totally different – a 'hot dog' stand!

Today, most of the 800 Polar Eskimos have their homes in the district's seven settlements, scattered along the strip of rocky coastline between Melville Bay and Robertson Fjord.

If Peary were able to visit them now, he might be surprised by the villages with their modern houses; particularly Qaanaaq, the largest, which has electricity, televisions, and a video library. But if he were to go out on the land he would still find the hunters dressed in furs, travelling across the sea ice by dog-sled, and using harpoons and other traditional hunting equipment. He would probably notice that the Primus stove had replaced the seal oil lamp, and that the sled lashings and the dogs' traces were of nylon instead of bearded seal skin. He might raise an eyebrow at the telescopic sights on some of the modern rifles, but on the whole he wouldn't find the hunting life so different from that of the early 1900s.

The reason that many of the 'old ways' still continue in Thule is largely due to the Polar Eskimos themselves. For it is their community's own hunting council that has taken measures like banning the use of snowmobiles, which are so widespread in the rest of the Arctic, and implementing restrictions on hunting from motor boats. In Thule today, an Inuit who goes hunting for narwhals in the summer must do so from a kayak using a traditional harpoon. These and numerous other hunting regulations were introduced in the belief that they would help to preserve the Polar Eskimo culture and conserve game for future generations of hunters.

The seasonal changes in the Arctic are dramatic and their effects more pronounced than in many other areas with a more temperate climate. The life of the Inuit has always been governed by the Arctic's seasons. From their understanding of the animals and their environment, different Inuit groups have evolved their own seasonal cycle, following the movements of the animals they hunt from one area to another.

The Long Arctic Winter

The blowing snow stung my face as I walked through Moriussaq village towards Ituku's home. It was late November, almost midday, and dark. The sun had set a month ago, marking the beginning of North Greenland's long polar winter.

The wind had been blowing relentlessly for three days now, keeping most of the settlement's 58 inhabitants indoors. The light in the windows from kerosene lamps and the occasional flicker of a flashlight as a figure scurried from one house to another, were the only signs of life. Outside Ituku's hut his team of huskies lay tightly curled in the snow, their backs to the wind and muzzles tucked under their bushy tails to protect them from the bitter cold.

I scrambled through the low entrance hall into the warm hut. Ituku was kneeling on the floor putting the finishing touches to a new harpoon, while his girlfriend, Panerak, was busy sewing a pair of sealskin *kamik* (boots) for their year-old son. 'Everyday there is wind,' said Ituku as he greeted me. He stood up and balanced the harpoon in his right hand in a throwing position. A smile of satisfaction spread across his face. He was pleased with it. In a few days, he explained, there would be light from the full moon and we would go out to hunt walrus.

Forty years old, Ituku is one of the more skilled Polar Eskimo hunters. He is a hard worker and a man who can't sit idly inside a house during fine weather. His ability as a hunter and his almost compelling need to be out and about are characteristics he probably inherited from his father, Qaivigarssuaq. Qaivigarssuaq is a legendary figure amongst the Polar Eskimos, a great hunter and a member of the Fifth Thule expedition, organised by the Danish ethnologist and explorer Knud Rasmussen. Between 1921 and 1924 they travelled by dog sled from Greenland right across the Canadian Arctic to Alaska, a journey of some 27,000 miles.

Three days later we were heading west across the sea ice. After a racing start out of Moriussaq the fourteen huskies had settled down to a steady trot. The weather couldn't have been better. It was cold -25°C, with not a breath of wind. The sky was clear, revealing a mass of stars and the full moon, which bathed the sea ice in light, giving us a visibility of twenty miles or more.

'Maybe later we will eat walrus meat,' said Ituku. He was in high spirits at the prospect of the hunt. For the Polar Eskimos a walrus is a prize catch, as a single animal can provide a ton or more of meat with a bonus of the ivory tusks that they can sell at the settlement store. But hunting a walrus is no easy task, particularly in the winter darktime, when the hunters often have to venture out onto dangerously thin ice in an attempt to harpoon them at their breathing holes.

The swish of the sled runners as they passed over the ice and the panting of the huskies were the only sounds. Once you are out of the villages, North Greenland in winter is a silent world. There may be the occasional call of a raven as it circles above you, but that is the only bird you are likely to hear. For the raven, ptarmigan and the snowy owl are the only birds that winter this far north, all the others flying south at the end of the Arctic summer.

After three hours sledding we reached Umivik, at the eastern tip of Saunders Island, and it was time for a tea break. We stopped near the shore by a small iceberg that was frozen fast by the sea ice. While I lit the kerosene Primus stove, Ituku walked over to the iceberg and chipped off a block of ice with his snow knife. For most of the year, water in North Greenland comes in 'block' form from icebergs produced by the region's countless glaciers. In the autumn small icebergs are often washed ashore close to the villages. After freeze up the Inuit rely on them for fresh drinking water.

While he waited for the water to boil, Ituku walked ashore to check a trap he had set previously for Arctic foxes, but he returned empty handed. Then, with our tea break over, Ituku untangled the traces of his dog-team, and we were on the move again, travelling along the sea ice with the island's craggy cliffs towering above us. We rounded a small headland and Ituku pointed out a line of fog suspended above the ice in the distance. 'Maybe there is open water there' he said. He was right, and a short while later we were standing at the edge of the ice. The wind of the previous days had blown all the ice out; in front of us open water blocked our way for as far as the eye could see. To hunt walrus now would be 'very difficult' Ituku explained as he scanned the open water. The Inuit language has no word for 'impossible.'

To add to our frustration we could hear the occasional deep grunts of walrus in the distance. *'Ajor!'* (sad) exclaimed Ituku, but he showed no other signs of disappointment. I have always been impressed by the ability of the Inuit to smile and remain cheerful in times of adversity. The life of a hunter like Ituku is continually governed by changes in the weather or snow and ice conditions. This could be why in the Inuit language there are dozens of words to describe different conditions of ice and snow. Ituku untangled the dogs' traces and, turning the sled, we set off back towards the mainland. At least the good weather had held.

An hour or so later the dogs suddenly began to run flat out, veering first to the left and then to the right, before coming to a dead stop. They had scented the fishy smell of a seal's breath as it surfaced at its Agdlo (breathing hole) in the sea ice. Ituku quickly jumped off the sled and walked in front of his team until he found the breathing hole. He knelt down on the ice and examined it. It was fresh – it had no ice covering it. He grabbed his harpoon and rifle and positioned himself by the hole, while I, as I had many times before, drove the dogs two hundred yards away in the hope it would fool the seal into thinking that Ituku was no longer near the breathing hole. Ituku waited motionless by the hole, rifle and harpoon at the ready. After fifteen minutes had passed without the seal surfacing it was obvious that our ploy wasn't going to work and Ituku gave up. It wasn't his day. The ice was thin and Ituku thought that the seal had probably seen his moonshadow through it.

On our way back Ituku decided to make a detour to the Manson Islands. He had set two nets under the ice there to catch seals and he wanted to check them. I brewed some tea while Ituku saw to his nets. Suddenly he let out a shriek of delight; he had caught two seals in one net. He wouldn't return home empty handed after all.

It was two in the morning when we finally reached Moriussaq. There were still lights shining from some of the houses and outside I could see figures moving around in the moonlight; not everyone was asleep. For Inuit hunting communities have no fixed regime for the day. Apart from catching the store open, time is of little importance. The Inuit sleep when they are tired and eat when they are hungry.

In the higher latitudes of the Arctic the sun sets at the end of October and isn't seen again above the horizon until the middle of February. One of the popular myths that exist about the Inuit is that they hibernate through this period of darkness. For an Inuit hunter with a family and twenty huskies to feed the need to provide meat is ever present, and he will continue to hunt throughout the year. Their hunting activities are limited during this time, not just by the darkness, but also by the ice and weather conditions. It is not a time of year when they make long hunting trips, relying more on game that is closer to home. In periods of bad weather, when they can't hunt, there is usually some work that needs doing at home, and when that is finished they will often pass the time by visiting other families. In the past the Inuit provided their own amusement, with traditional pastimes like drum singing and a variety of games from trials of strength to cat's cradle. In the modern Arctic these have largely been replaced by television and video recorders. Winter is a good time for carving. Inuit soapstone and ivory carvings, particularly those by the Canadian Inuit, are much in demand by collectors. Some of the settlements, such as Cape Dorset and Baker Lake, have achieved an international reputation for the quality of their art. While for some of the Inuit carving has become a full time occupation, for others it remains just a useful way of raising hard cash during times when they are unable to hunt.

The women, too, keep themselves busy. A hunter's wife will seldom have time on her hands. Apart from looking after the children and doing all the usual domestic chores, she must make and maintain the family's fur clothing as well as cleaning and drying all the skins her husband brings home. Cleaning a seal skin is an art which involves scraping off all the blubber with an *ulu* (a round-bladed woman's knife). The tricky part is doing it without making a hole in the skin! If she is married to a good hunter, that alone will keep her busy for most of the time. Though hunting is considered to be 'man's work' by the Inuit, it is not unheard of for women to hunt. In Baker Lake, in the Central Canadian North, I met one woman who, after her husband had died, took over his role as provider, keeping her own trap line and hunting caribou as well as looking after her children. But on the whole women get involved with lighter forms of hunting, such as fishing and catching birds.

Though February is the month that brings back the sun, it doesn't bring back its warmth. It is the coldest month of the year, with temperatures down as low as -40°C or less. While the Arctic's animals were well provided by nature with thick fur coats to survive these extreme temperatures, man was never designed to survive in this environment. He has, however, adapted remarkably well, for over thousands of years the Inuit have perfected the art of keeping warm in the severest of Arctic weather. Though there are regional variations in their dress, the basic principle is the same throughout the North – a double layer of skin clothes; the inside layer worn with the fur facing inward and the outer layer worn with the fur facing out. In the Canadian North, winter clothing is made predominantly from caribou skin, its hollow hairs offering excellent insulation, while in North Greenland there are more variations, with the skins of seal, polar bear, caribou, and Arctic fox all being combined to make a set of winter clothes.

As yet the Inuit have found no modern substitute to match fur clothing for warmth and durability. While in a settlement an Inuit hunter might be dressed in the latest blue denim with a parka over the top, but the chances are that when he goes out on the land he will dress in traditional furs.

Just as unstable weather frequently follows the disappearance of the sun in October, the same happens after the sun's return. February is often stormy. If there is one aspect of the weather that the Inuit have the greatest respect for it's the wind. In the Arctic a winter storm can begin with surprising suddenness, whipping up the snow and reducing visibility from thirty miles to thirty feet in a matter of moments. With no trees in the Arctic to break its progress, the power of the wind racing across the tundra is awesome. It can break up and blow out vast areas of sea ice, and the chilling effect on the human body at low temperatures can be lethal.

Although the Inuit can often predict these big winds by the cloud formation, the nature of their lifestyle inevitably results in their being caught out in storms from time to time. In a big wind hunters will try to shelter by building an igloo or placing bricks of snow around a tent, but sometimes they have no alternative but to keep moving. Their skill at navigating in these conditions has always amazed me.

One time, in early March, I was out in Melville Bay with a group of Inuit hunters after seals. It was getting dark and we were about to make camp on the sea ice when the wind began to blow. To begin with it was just a few gusts, but within minutes we had a storm on our hands. The hunters were worried that the ice might blow out, and decided to seek shelter in a hunter's hut at Cape York, some fifteen miles away. Conditions were horrendous; the wind made our eyes water and the cold froze the tears to our lashes. Visibility was down to only a few yards and at times the blown snow almost concealed the dogs pulling the sled.

After four hours of sledding I was convinced we were lost. We seemed to be travelling into a void and we had no compass or any other navigational aid. A short while later I suddenly caught sight of what I thought was a star directly ahead of us. It turned out to be a light from the window of the hunters' hut at Cape York. We were safe. It had been a remarkable piece of navigation, and I was impressed. But how had they done it? The answer, I discovered later, was that they had used the *sastrugi* (grooves carved in the surface of the snow by the prevailing winds) to guide them.

The Arctic's winter weather does have its advantages for the Inuit. The snow on the land is hardened by the cold and the wind, making it easier for a hunter to sled across in his search for caribou. Vast areas of the sea will be frozen too, giving the Inuit a larger area to hunt in than at any other time of the year. After the return of the sun in February, the days lengthen fast. In the higher areas of the Arctic the sun stays above the horizon for 20 minutes more each day.

The sea ice closer to the settlements is too thick in February for setting seal nets, and the hunters must go further afield now to hunt seals at breathing holes or at leads in the sea ice.

It's a time of year when the Inuit traditionally make longer hunting journeys. For the Inuit in North Greenland it is the time to hunt *Nanok* - the polar bear. Polar bears in this part of the world are hunted throughout the fall and winter months, but it tends to be only when a hunter comes across them or, as happens occasionally, one wanders into a hunting camp or a settlement.

It is only towards the end of the winter that the hunters make these long journeys far out onto the ice of Melville Bay and Smith Sound specifically for polar bear. It is usually the more successful hunters with the stronger dog teams that go, for these trips can last a month or more of gruelling travel over difficult ice, sledding all day and camping on the ice at night. They hunt seals along the way, food for their dogs and themselves, but it's a polar bear they are hoping for. Every so often they will stop to climb an iceberg, using it as a vantage point to scan the surrounding sea ice for any sign of a bear. The search continues; day after day it's the same, until they come across fresh bear tracks. Then the excitement starts; they follow the tracks, sometimes for hours; suddenly they'll catch sight of the bear in the distance. In a frenzy of excitement they unlash the sleds, discarding everything that isn't absolutely essential, to lighten the load. Speed is of the essence now as they set off after the bear. The hunters don't speak; using only sign language and the raven's call to attract one another's attention without alerting the bear. As they close in on their quarry, the traces of the best dogs are slashed with a snow knife and, free from the sled, they run flat out across the ice after the bear. Sometimes the bear will escape by swimming a stretch of open water but, if the men are lucky, the dogs will catch up with the bear and harass it, barking and dashing in to bite it, trying to dodge the powerful swing of its forepaws, holding it at bay until the hunters get close. There is the crack of a rifle and the bear crumples, dead, onto the ice. The Inuit are jubilant, the ultimate hunt is over. Today, if two hunters return with a polar bear to share between them after a month-long trip, they will be pleased.

Though polar bear meat is a delicacy amongst the Polar Eskimos, and there is a certain amount of machismo and tradition involved in hunting bears, it is the skin that is the main motivation behind the hunt. The hunters could earn a lot of money by selling them, but few polar bear skins ever leave the Thule district of Northwest Greenland district to end up gracing the homes of the wealthy. Instead, they are cut up and used to make trousers, as they have been for more than a thousand years.

Polar bear trousers are more than just part of a traditional costume. They have proved to be unbeatable protection against North Greenland's severe Arctic climate, which is why the Polar Eskimos continue to wear them despite the market value of a polar bear skin making the trousers worth around $1,000 a pair!

Spring without Flowers

April marks the beginning of spring in the high Arctic. A very different spring to that experienced in lower latitudes, for the temperature stays well below zero centigrade, the sea remains frozen, snow still covers the land and there is certainly no sign of any flowers.
Despite this, there are changes happening that will gradually transform the Arctic towards summer. The sun is higher in the sky and you can feel its warmth at last. The days are becoming progressively longer, and by the end of the month the sun will remain above the horizon twenty four hours a day until late August.

If there is one single event that heralds the approach of spring in the high Arctic it is the arrival of the snow buntings in mid April. These chirpy little songbirds are usually the first birds to arrive from the south each year, and the Inuit have a great deal of affection for them.

It is not just birds that are on the move at this time, but animals as well. The caribou begin their spring migration and the walruses swim northwards, following the receding ice edge. It is a time too when the Inuit travel. Not just to hunt, but to visit friends and relatives in other settlements. In Northwest Greenland family get-togethers often take place at Easter and at the confirmation ceremonies which are held a few weeks later. For today, most Inuit follow one form or another of Christianity, with mainly Protestants and Catholics in the Canadian North, while Lutheranism has a virtual monopoly in Greenland.

The missionaries were very effective in 'converting' the Inuit to Christianity, though this was often done with insensitivity and a lack of understanding of the native culture. An elderly Inuit man in Northwest Greenland told me how, when he was young, a missionary visited his home just after his wife had given birth to a baby. On seeing a blue mark at the base of the baby's spine, the missionary had gone into a rage, shouting at the Inuit couple that they were bad people for beating their child. The couple were too frightened to offer any explanation. In fact, the blue mark at the base of the baby's spine was not a bruise at all, but a mark that every Inuit baby is born with, a legacy of their Mongolian heritage.

No people on earth are kinder or more gentle to their children than the Inuit. They adore them, and treat them with respect. This may be because the children are often named after respected members of the community who have recently died. The Inuit believe that the spirit of the dead person then lives on in the child.

Even though most of North Greenland's Polar Eskimos follow the Lutheran faith, many of the 'old beliefs' in shamans, spirits and taboos still linger on, albeit concealed under a veneer of Christianity. I had an experience of this a few years ago while travelling with the hunter, Ituku.

We had been out hunting in Melville Bay when bad weather forced us to take refuge in Savissivik, the most southerly village in the Thule district. We were sitting in the home of one of the Savissivik hunters drinking coffee when an old man with only one tooth came in and sat down. He asked me for liquor. I told him that I had none. Then he turned and spoke to Ituku. I couldn't understand the conversation but Ituku looked visibly shocked; he stood up and walked out of the hut. I followed him outside to find out what the matter was, but Ituku would say no more than that the old man was a 'bad man', so I dropped the subject.

The next day the weather had improved and so we left to continue our hunt. Melville Bay is notorious for its difficult ice conditions, but during the next ten days it seemed that we had more than our fair share. We had to cross ridges of pressure ice over six feet high in places, and stretches of open water seemed constantly to be blocking our way. All this culminated in a storm which forced us to take refuge on an iceberg while the sea ice broke up around us. Despite this the hunt was successful, Ituku got a polar bear and several seals. He was in good spirits as we headed for home so I asked him again what the old man in Savissivik had said to him. This time he was more forthcoming; the old man had asked for liquor and told Ituku that unless we gave him some, we would have 'bad ice' out in Melville Bay. 'Some people say he's an *angakoq* (shaman)', Ituku added, and he laughed, but it was an uncomfortable laugh.

April is also the start of the breeding season in the high Arctic. The ringed seal, the most common seal found in the region, gives birth to its young in snow caves on the ice. The raven is the first bird to breed, and by mid-April some will be sitting on a clutch of eggs despite the temperature still being well below freezing.

By the beginning of May the sun begins to make its presence felt and the Arctic starts to warm up. The sea no longer freezes, an ice edge forms which will gradually retreat towards the land, and the increasing amount of open water gives the sea birds a greater area in which to feed. Glaucous gulls, kittiwakes, fulmers and guillemots arrive in ever increasing numbers. The Arctic winter's spell of silence is broken.

In North Greenland it is the arrival of one seabird in particular that the Inuit most look forward to - the *dovkie* (little auk). Each May they arrive in their millions to nest amongst the rocky slopes of the district's coastline. These squat little sea birds are a delicacy amongst the Polar Eskimos, and news of their arrival spreads like wildfire around the settlements. Catching them, though, is something of an art. The Inuit must first conceal themselves behind a rock and then, using a long-handled net known as an *ipu*, try to sweep the birds out of the air as they fly past. Camps quickly form at the dovkie colonies and a holiday atmosphere prevails. Catching dovkie's isn't restricted to the men – it's a type of hunting that the whole family can try their hand at. I have even seen huskies jump into the air and catch the occasional bird that flies too close.

Although the Inuit like to eat dovkies fresh, it is as *kiviaq* that they earn their reputation as a delicacy. Kiviaq is prepared by placing the freshly-killed birds inside a sealskin which is then sewn shut and buried under stones for six months or more. A favourite food for festive occasions, kiviaq is the Polar Eskimo equivalent of cheese and, to most outsiders, an acquired taste.

Traditionally, the Inuit diet comprised mainly meat and fat, with fish, bird's eggs and berries available at certain times of the year. Although many of the stores in today's Arctic stock a wide array of convenience and junk foods, in most hunting communities meat and fat remain the basis of the Inuit diet. In the Polar Eskimo settlements of Northwest Greenland, seal is the most commonly eaten meat, followed by walrus, whale and polar bear. That might sound rather a very limited menu, but like most cultures, the Inuit have their favourite cuts and different ways of preparing meat to give it variety. Seal, for example, may be eaten raw, boiled, dried or as *igunaq* (decayed like kiviaq), depending on the cut and the circumstances.

Nowadays, in North America and Europe we are told that a high fibre diet of cereals, milk products, a little meat but plenty of fruit and vegetables is the way to eat healthily. This would tend to suggest that the Inuit diet based on meat and fat couldn't be anything other than unhealthy. This is not the case, for it is possible to keep perfectly healthy on a meat and fat diet. Vitamins don't necessarily have to come from fruit and vegetables – some meats contain high vitamin levels too. For example, both raw seal liver and whale skin contain up to 38mgs of vitamin C per 100 grams, roughly the same as grapefruit. Medical surveys carried out on the Inuit have revealed low cholesterol levels, and the incidence of heart disease, diabetes and cancer is low.

Many of the diet-related diseases that now effect the Inuit are the result of imported foods. Most noticeable is the tooth decay that has resulted from a high sugar intake, particularly prevalent amongst children, though it has effected older people too. I can remember travelling with Kaugunak, an elderly hunter from Siorapaluk in Northwest Greenland. While we stopped to brew tea one time, Kaugunak produced a piece of *quaq* (frozen raw meat). I watched admiringly as he bit off and ate great chunks of it, while I barely managed to leave an impression of my teeth on the surface. 'I wish I had teeth like his', I thought to myself at the time. A few weeks later a dentist visited Siorapaluk and I was allowed to photograph at the surgery he held in the village school. One of his first patients was Kaugunak, who walked in, sat down in the chair and removed his set of dentures. To this day I don't know how he managed to eat that frozen meat.

In the late spring, when it becomes warmer, families will often leave their settlement homes and move to hunting camps out on the land. In the past the Inuit lived at hunting camps the entire year but, although there are some families, mainly in the Canadian North, that still do, this is now very rare. For most of the Inuit nowadays, hunting camps are essentially something for the spring and summer.

In the Thule district of Northwest Greenland, the schools break up at the end of May so the children can travel out to hunting camps with their parents. It is looked on as part of their education, for they will learn about hunting and life on the land. It's a pleasant time to be at a camp. The weather is warm and the snow begins to melt on the land. Ringed seals enlarge their breathing holes and haul themselves up onto the ice to bask in the warm sunshine.

The Inuit have to adopt different techniques to hunt these basking seals. Above all they need camouflage, for the sea ice offers little cover to conceal a hunter. The Polar Eskimos use a white linen screen mounted on a small wooden sled. The rifle is lashed to the sled with the end of the barrel just protruding through the screen. The hunter stalks the seal by pushing the screen in front of him. Every time the seal looks up, the hunter stops, for if the seal sees him it will quickly disappear down its breathing hole. The hunter will usually try to get as close as possible before shooting, for he must kill the seal outright; a wounded seal will often still manage to escape into the water.

At this time of year the Inuit will often travel to the ice edge to hunt, sometimes hunting from the ice itself and retrieving their prey with kayaks. Later on, when the ice edge comes closer to the land, they will often hunt from boats with outboard motors which they take to the ice edge by sled. They are remarkably skilled at manoeuvring boats amongst ice floes, where the gaps of open water are constantly opening and closing.

Even more impressive is their ability to fix the outboard motors when they break down, as they do from time to time. They often don't have the necessary spare part and so they improvise. I was out in a boat with an Inuit hunter one time when the starter cord broke. He had no suitable nylon cord so he trimmed a piece of bearded seal skin thong until it was the right size and used that. I don't know how long it lasted, but at least it got us back safely.

Their mechanical skills extend to snowmobiles too. In the early days these machines were notoriously unreliable, and nicknamed a 'drive out and walk home' in some parts of the Arctic. By and large, the Inuit hunters are very tough on their machines, and drive them hard. Inevitably, they break down, usually in the middle of nowhere, but somehow or other the Inuit have that magic knack of getting them going again.

Just how ingenious they can be as mechanics I discovered one March when I hitched a ride with an Inuit hunter returning from an outpost camp on Baffin Island to the settlement of Igloolik, a journey of just over 100 miles. It was a cold day, around -36°C and, from the outset, the snowmobile played up. We covered no more than a mile at a time before the engine would cut out. After a while I began to get a little anxious at the prospect of just the two of us being miles from anywhere with a broken-down snowmobile. I began to wish we were travelling by dog-sled. It might have been slower, but at least dogs don't break down.

After the engine had cut out for the fifth time, I decided to use the opportunity to answer the call of nature and get rid of some of the mugs of tea I had drunk before leaving. I was in the process of unbuttoning my fly when my companion called out to me 'Not on the ice!' and then, pointing at the snowmobile, he added, 'On the carburettor'. I did as instructed and the snowmobile started at the first attempt and kept going until we reached Igloolik. I later discovered that urinating on a snowmobile's carburettor to warm it was a standard ploy used by the Inuit hunters of the Eastern Canadian Arctic.

Hunting Under the Midnight Sun

June is the month when the higher areas of the Arctic undergo their most dramatic change. With the intense sunlight during the day the temperature climbs well above freezing, and the thaw sets in. A new sound is heard – running water – as gushing melt streams cross the land.

Though in some areas, where it has drifted deep, the snow remains until July, it will melt away from most of the land during June. Within three weeks of the snow disappearing the tundra is transformed from a pallid, greyish-brown to a blaze of colour by a vast carpet of millions of tiny flowering plants.

The speed at which the Arctic changes at this time is amazing. It is almost as though there is a race on, and to a certain extent there is. It's a race against time. For summers in the high Arctic are extremely short, with a growing season, when the mean temperature is above freezing, of only three months. The twenty-four-hour sunlight does compensate, however, by enabling photosynthesis to take place throughout this period, without being interrupted by darkness.

Also affected by the urgency to reproduce are the large numbers of migratory birds that fly north to the Arctic each spring. June is the month when most species lay their eggs. At the bird cliffs it seems as though every horizontal ledge is crammed with glaucous gulls, kittiwakes, fulmers and guillemots, while inland the air is full of bird song and the wind carries the eerie cry of the loon across the tundra from distant lakes.

In Northwest Greenland, the arrival of such great numbers of sea birds provides the Inuit with an additional source of food. Though they eat gulls, dovkies, guillemots, eider ducks and the occasional fulmer, it is the eggs that are a delicacy.

A high spot of early summer for the Polar Eskimos is the one day each year at the end of June when they are allowed to take the eggs and down from the district's eider duck colonies. The local Hunter's Council sets the date, which is always early enough in the breeding season for the eiders to lay a second clutch of eggs.

I joined the villagers of Moriussaq one time for their annual raid on the nearby eider duck colonies. There was a party feeling as virtually the whole village piled into four boats and we set off towards the Three Sisters Bess, a small group of flat islands which have long been a favourite breeding ground of the eiders. The noise of our arrival had cleared all but the broodiest of the birds from the island. Once everyone was safely ashore, men, women and children lined up at one end of the colony armed with bags to collect the down and plastic buckets for the eggs. Then, on the count of three, everyone set off at a run in search of the nests, followed by shrieks of delight from the children whenever they found one. Once the colony had been thoroughly searched, the eggs and down were carried back to the boats and we set off for another colony on the Manson Islands. There, the whole procedure was repeated. When that colony had been searched as well, everyone gathered their eggs and down together; Primus stoves were lit and a 'boiled egg party' began, with everyone gorging themselves on the large, rich eggs. Some of those not eaten would be taken back to the village, while others were cached under rocks on the island for eating at a later date. The down would be sold to the trading store. On the way back to Moriussaq, one of the hunters turned to me and said, 'It's a shame you don't have your wife with you this time', and everyone in the boat laughed, for the Polar Eskimos believe that eggs are an aphrodisiac.

Throughout June, the sea ice gradually deteriorates. The leads begin to widen and the snow becomes soft, making it hard for the dogs to pull a sled. Then the Inuit begin to travel more by night, when the sun is lower in the sky, and frosts still harden the snow. Later on in the month water begins to build up on the surface of the ice and at night sharp ice crystals form which can lacerate the dogs' feet. The Inuit have to tie improvised *kamik* (boots) onto the dogs' feet to protect them.

Once into July, the water on the ice may be two feet deep or more; holes begin to develop, and the leads become wider and wider. Travelling by dog sled at this time is a wet and miserable experience. Hunting on the sea ice usually ceases, and the only sledding that is done is by families travelling to camps where they will spend the summer.

Some will trek inland and camp by lakes where they can catch Arctic char, while others will remain at the coast, waiting for the ice to go out. It can be a long wait. In sheltered areas of Northwest Greenland the ice will often remain until the first week of August. This can be a lean time for the hunters, when the ice is too bad to sled on but still too thick to use a kayak or boat. Often it can be frustrating for them too, for they will be able to see seals basking on the ice or narwhals swimming in a lead but be unable to hunt them. For the duration of the summer the huskies become redundant. Tethered out on the tundra, they laze in the warmth of the summer sunshine.

The hunters will often use this time to prepare for summer hunting. There is usually something that needs doing, from repairing a hole in a tent to making a new kayak. The Inuit kayak is one of the most graceful and efficient craft ever designed by man. In former times it was used by Inuit groups right across the Arctic, but nowadays glass-fibre boats and canoes with outboard motors have largely replaced it. Greenland is one of the few areas left where it is still in common use as a hunting craft.

The Inuit kayak isn't built to a standard size. It's rather like a tailor- made suit, constructed to fit the physique of the owner. It is impressive the way the Inuit make these fine-lined craft without plans, and often without another kayak to copy from, just by eye and using the minimum of tools.

I first saw this some years ago when I was at a hunting camp in early summer. One day, just as the ice was beginning to get bad, an elderly man called Inutuk arrived by dog sled. Along with his tent and supplies for the summer he had four long planks of wood lashed onto his sled. As he began to work with the wood I asked him what he was going to make. 'A kayak for my grandson,' he replied. To most enthusiasts equipped with an array of the latest electrical tools this would still have been a lengthy and ambitious project. Inutuk made it look easy, using only a saw, a snow knife and a small hand drill. In just ten days he transformed the four planks into an elegant kayak frame. For the watertight covering he used five sealskins, having prepared them by removing the fur, then soaking them in sea water for several days. The skins had to be sewn onto the kayak frame while they were still wet. All the women of the camp joined in to help and a lively sewing party began which lasted late into the night. Nowadays most of the kayaks are covered with canvas or plastic sheeting.

By the beginning of August there is a great feeling of anticipation along the shores of Inglefield Sound. This sixty-mile-long stretch of water becomes the centre of the hunters' attention as they wait for an easterly wind to blow the ice out to sea. For as soon as the ice breaks up narwhals enter the sound to feed and give birth to their young.

The narwhal is one of the smaller toothed whales and grows to around fifteen feet in length. The whalers of the 19th century called it the 'sea unicorn' because of the long, ivory tooth that males have protruding from their heads. The exact purpose of this tooth, which can grow up to eight feet in length, isn't known, though it is thought that it plays a role in social dominance.

For an Inuit hunter a narwhal is a valuable catch, providing large quantities of meat, blubber, and *magtaq* (skin), which is a delicacy. The ivory teeth are a bonus that can be sold. Traditionally, the muscle sinew was stretched and dried for use as strong sewing thread, though dental floss, which has similar qualities, has superseded it in Northwest Greenland.

On occasions, narwhals enter Inglefield Sound in great numbers. One of the most spectacular sights that I have ever seen in the Arctic I witnessed one summer while camped on a headland at the end of the sound. I was awakened at two in the morning by the sound of narwhals and I quickly scrambled from my tent. The water was flat calm and the warm light of the early morning sunshine was reflected in its surface. Suddenly, close to the shore, the mirror surface of the water was broken by a narwhal's tooth; then behind it other narwhals surfaced. That was only the beginning. They were followed by more and more. I watched entranced for an hour as pod after pod swam by. How many were there? It would be impossible to say exactly, but there were certainly hundreds. A spectacular sight, but by no means unique. In 1985 scientists counted more than 4,000 narwhals in Inglefield Sound on a single day.

Although at times there may be great numbers of narwhals, catching them is never easy. A hunter must get close enough to a whale that has surfaced to harpoon it by hand from a kayak, a technique that has been used for centuries. Hunting narwhals is essentially a 'waiting game'. There is no telling when narwhals might appear, and the hunters keep a constant watch day and night, but days or even weeks sometimes go by with no sign of a whale.

Camps form at traditional sites all along the coast of Inglefield Sound. These are places which have a good vantage point from which to scan the water and where narwhals often come close to the shore. Inuit summer hunting camps are lively, happy places, with almost a holiday atmosphere. The children especially enjoy them. It's warm, the sun shines day and night, so they can play outside until they drop from exhaustion. Nobody says 'it's bedtime'. For them there is so much to do – there are fish to catch, stones to skim and birds' nests to be found. Many of the games the children play imitate the activities of their parents, which helps prepare them for their adult roles in life. When a hunter returns to camp after being out hunting in his kayak he is likely to have a young son anxious to get in it so he can paddle and pretend to harpoon a narwhal.

For the adults too it's a relaxed time to enjoy the company of friends and relatives. A time when it's pleasant to sit out in the sunshine and listen to the sounds of the Arctic in summer. But, primarily, summer camps are about hunting.

It is the cry 'Qilalugaq! Qilalugaq!' (Narwhal! Narwhal!) that brings a hunting camp instantly to life day or night. Hunters will grab binoculars and climb up to a vantage point to see how many narwhals there are and in what direction they are heading. If it looks as though they will pass reasonably close to the camp, the hunters will rush to launch their kayaks, paddling quickly out into the sound to position themselves in what they hope will be the narwhals path. Then they will wait motionless in their kayaks, while the women watch from the shore. Only if a narwhal surfaces close to one of the kayaks will the hunter give chase, paddling flat out, pursuing it until he is close enough. Then, in one fluid motion, he will lay the paddle on the deck, raise his harpoon and throw. If the harpoon finds its mark the hunter will quickly jettison his *avataq* (an inflated sealskin buoy attached to the harpoon line) from the rear deck. The whale dives, pulling the avataq below the surface. Then once again the hunters must wait, but sooner or later the whale must surface again to breathe. When the avataq reappears, it shows the hunters where the whale is, and they paddle after it to try to harpoon it for the second time, before it is finally killed with a lance or a large calibre rifle, and sinks dead beneath the waves.

The dead narwhal is then hauled to the surface and the hunters attach avataqs to it to give it buoyancy before triumphantly towing it back to shore. There the *magtaq* (skin) is carefully flensed from the dead animal before the carcase is butchered and divided up into hunting shares. There is a tradition among the Inuit that everyone who participates in a hunt is entitled to a share. Usually the size of the share is dependent on the role the person played in the hunt, though in most cases it is only necessary to touch the dead animal to receive a share of the meat. This tradition ensures that the old and less able members of the community are always provided for.

Often, the hunters will go out in their kayaks after sighting narwhals only to return empty handed. On some occasions, they will spend many hours at a time waiting in their frail craft. When whales aren't around the hunters go out after seals. They need as much meat as they can get, and anything not eaten at the camp will be cached. The summer draws to a close all too soon, and they will need meat for the coming winter.

The Shortening Days to Freeze Up

August is the month when the birds leave the high Arctic, migrating south to warmer climates before the long Arctic winter once more grips the land. Young birds only a few weeks old have long, tiring journeys ahead of them. Most remarkable are the Arctic terns, which will fly some 12,000 miles to the Antarctic. By the end of the month the shoreline and the bird cliffs will once again be silent. Mammals, too, prepare to migrate; the caribou gather and begin to head south to their winter pastures. The animals that will over winter in the Arctic prepare themselves for the severe temperatures to come by building up reserves of fat and growing thick fur.

The sun begins to sink lower in the sky, and by the end of August it will set again at night. It's colder and, as the frosts become more severe, the leaves of the plants change, providing the tundra with a vibrant cover of red and gold, a last burst of colour before winter. But before the tundra is once again enveloped by snow, it yields a valuable supply of food. For August is the month that the berries on the plants ripen and the Arctic abounds with crowberries, bilberries, cloudberries and mountain cranberries. Birds, Arctic foxes, even polar bears eat large amounts of these berries, and so too does man. The Inuit particularly relish crowberries, which they either eat on their own or with fresh seal blubber.

By the beginning of September in Northwest Greenland the first snows have settled on the land. Ice begins to form on inland lakes and in sheltered bays along the coast. The hunting is usually good at this time; seals are often plentiful, and the hunters make the most of this last opportunity to accumulate meat and skins before the traditionally lean time of winter darkness. Some of the skins will be used to make winter clothes, while the better ones are usually sold to the trading store.

The most serious threat to the Inuit culture in recent years has come from the emotional outcry against the annual baby harp seal cull in Canada and the resulting import ban on seal products imposed by the European Economic Community. The knock-on effect of this was to destroy almost totally the market for all types of sealskin, including that of the ringed seal, which is the most numerous to be found in the Arctic and on which the Inuit depend. During the 1970s a fine sealskin may have fetched $60 or more at auction. By 1985 the price had slumped to $5. The collapse of the sealskin market has brought hardship to many of the North's native communities, where employment possibilities for the Inuit are few, and for most the only real alternative to hunting is to live on a government handout.

Selling sealskins is one of the few means Inuit hunters have of raising cash to cover the cost of their needs – everything from toilet paper to ammunition. Living in the Arctic is very expensive, largely because of the difficulty of getting supplies to many of the isolated northern communities. In the high Arctic supply ships can only reach the settlements during the few weeks of summer when they are ice-free.

Once into October, the shortening days and the falling temperatures make the closeness of winter felt. This is an exceptionally beautiful time in the high Arctic, the low sun bathing the new ice and snow in a soft, warm light. The shortness of the days is compensated for by the long Arctic twilight. The sea ice forms quickly now when the wind drops. The hunters continue to go out in their boats, driving channels through the ice to reach the open sea. The days when they can continue to hunt from boats are numbered. Each time they go out it becomes harder. One October, I watched a hunter returning to the village of Moriussaq. He anchored his 20-foot wooden boat and got into a small dinghy. It then took him over half an hour of battling to manoeuvre the dinghy through 75 yards of ice to reach the shore. The next day he went out to his boat again, but this time he was able to walk out to it across the ice. It was time to bring the boats ashore.

Although the approach of the long period of winter darkness brings a sombre mood to the Inuit communities, there is also an air of excitement and anticipation as the sea ice thickens. Inevitably there is a period when there is too much ice to travel by boat but not enough to sled on, and hunters use this time to prepare their winter hunting equipment, so that, when the ice is finally thick enough, they will be ready. There is prestige to be gained by being the first to go hunting by dog sled on the new ice. The hunters might be prepared, but it often comes as a surprise to the huskies, who are faced with hard work again after four months of inactivity. The dogs are out of condition and teamwork is missing. Fights often break out, dissolving the team into a ball of snarling fur and making progress chaotic and slow.

In Northwest Greenland most hunters will use twelve to fourteen dogs in a team, running them in a fan formation. Some hunters may have as many as twenty-five, fifteen or sixteen that they run in their team and perhaps ten puppies and immature dogs too young to haul a sled. For the Polar Eskimos a large team of big dogs is a prized possession, and as much a status symbol as an expensive car is in other societies. Only a good hunter is able to provide enough meat to keep a large number of dogs.

As soon as the ice is thick enough, the hunters will set weighted nets suspended under the ice to catch seals. These nets, they hope, will provide them with meat during the dark time ahead, when it is often difficult for them even to find a breathing hole, let alone harpoon a seal. A hunter will probably set several nets in different places which have proved reliable in the past. Even so, they are always a gamble. One net may provide several seals each week while another only a few yards away may be continually empty. Setting nets at this time is risky because the ice is still thin and a storm could blow it out at any time, taking all the hunters' nets with it.

Storms are common at this time of year and can curtail the hunting. The Inuit accept bad weather as just another feature of the Arctic that is beyond their control. While at a hunting camp at Narssaarssuk we had strong winds that lasted three days. I was eager to be travelling again, and ended up pacing the floor for most of the time while the hunters slept, only getting up occasionally for food. 'How can you sleep for so long?' I asked Ituku during a brief waking moment. He shrugged and said, 'The wind carries sleep'. I thought back to the times in the summer when I had been hunting with Ituku for 72 hours without a break and how I had longed for him to say that it was time to get some sleep.

The days shorten rapidly now until sunrise merges into sunset. In Moriussaq the sun is last seen on October 29th, but even when it has set for the winter the sky still glows pink in the middle of the day for a couple of weeks. But all too soon even this comforting reminder of the sun's presence is gone, leaving only the moonlight to relieve the total darkness.

Facing page: Itakusuk Kristiansen, frosted up at -35°C.

Winter

Above: poised with his harpoon at the ready, a hunter waits at a seal's breathing hole. Facing page: (top) the moonlight of a January day illuminates a small iceberg frozen fast into sea ice (photograph © 1981 Time-Life Books B.V. from the *Peoples of the Wild* series), and the low winter sun sets beyond a husky (bottom) in Melville Bay. Overleaf: light from a kerosene lamp shines through the snow bricks of an igloo as an Inuit hunter prepares to camp for the night.

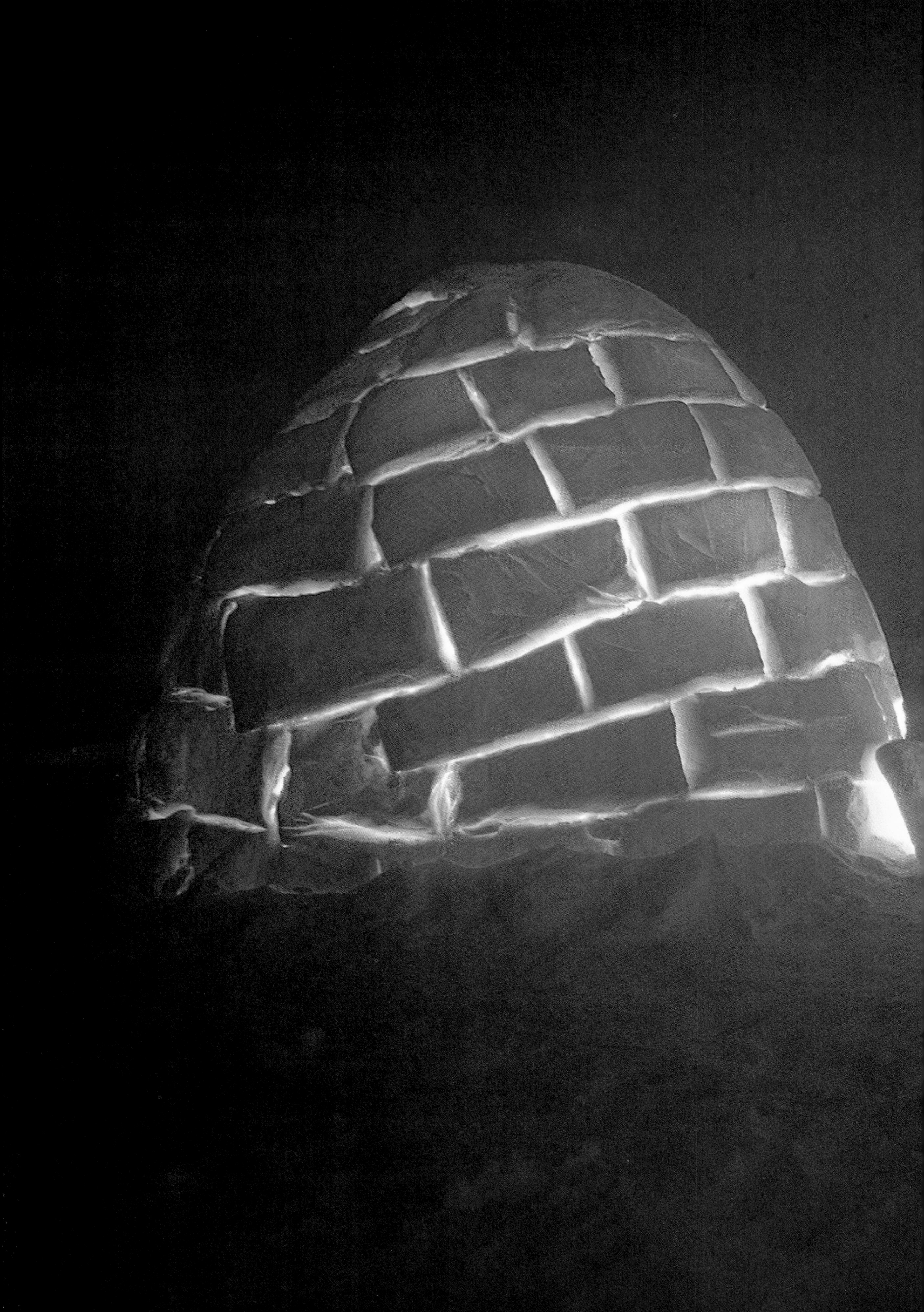

Facing page and top left: young Inuit girls, warmly wrapped in caribou skin clothes, and (top right) Augustine Taqqaugaq, all from Igloolik, Northwest Territories, and (above) Kaugunak Kissuk from Siorapaluk. Above right: Lars Nielsen from Savissivik preparing his homework by the light of a kerosene lamp. Overleaf: with a canvas tent erected over his sled, Ituku prepares to camp for the night on the sea ice in Melville Bay.

Facing page: in the golden glow of a low sun, Mamarut Kristiansen untangles the traces of his dogs and, (this page) using building bricks of snow, Avataq Henson builds an igloo as shelter during a hunting expedition. Overleaf: the welcoming lights of the village of Moriussaq during the winter dark time.

Facing page: (top) hunters relaxing in a hut at Cape York and (bottom) the interior of an Inuit outpost camp on Baffin Island, Northwest Territories. Below: Panerak using her teeth to soften a piece of sealskin while Ituku holds their son, and (bottom) Inuit hunters passing the time during bad weather by playing cards in a hut at Cape York.

Facing page: a harp seal carefully surfaces in mush ice and (top) Jens Danielsen stands on a pinnacle of ice to scan the surrounding sea ice of Melville Bay, while Ituku (above) prepares to harpoon a bearded seal in a lead near Igunaq.

Facing page: Inuit family at an outpost camp on Baffin Island. Top: Jens Danielsen shoots at a seal from the ice edge near Savissivik and (above) Ituku prepares to untangle the traces of his dog-team while out hunting near the Manson Islands, Northwest Greenland. Overleaf: Kaviganguak Kissuk preparing to position a snow brick while building an igloo.

TEAM YAMAHA
POLICE

Top: dog sleds at sunset near Cape York. Above: an Inuit hunter climbs an iceberg to scan the surrounding sea ice for polar bears, Melville Bay. Facing page: despite a temperature of -30°C, a hunter (top) prepares to use his kayak at the ice edge near Savissivik and Ituku (bottom) leads his dog team down onto the sea ice at Moriussaq. Overleaf: Inuit hunters untangle the traces of their dogs during a rest stop while out hunting in Melville Bay.

Top: a polar bear on the sea ice of Hudson Bay and (facing page) plunging into a lead in a bid to escape the Inuit hunters and their dogs. Above: Jens Danielsen guides his sled over a stretch of rough pressure ice while hunting polar bears in Melville Bay. Overleaf: a procession of dog sleds makes its way through deep snow on the sea ice near Cape York.

Facing page: (bottom) Inuit hunters with their dog sleds near Cape Atholl, and (top) a hunter untangling the traces of his dog team during a break in a sled trip. Below: the hunter Ituku prepares to skin a polar bear caught in Melville Bay, and (bottom) hunters meet while travelling across the frozen sea near Savissavik and stop to exchange news.

Facing page top: anticipation among the pack as Ituku feeds seal meat to his dog team at Cape York. Atop gleaming mounds of sculptured ice, hunters (facing page bottom) scan the surrounding sea ice for polar bears from an iceberg in Melville Bay. Below: Avataq Henson uses his kayak to retrieve a seal he has shot from the ice edge near Moriussaq, and (bottom) an Inuit woman cleans some Greenland halibut she has just caught. At -30°C the fish were deep frozen in minutes.

Facing page: to ensure a perfect fit, Kaviganguak Kissuk (top) uses his knife to trim the snow bricks of the igloo he is building, while Augustine Taqqaugaq (bottom) prepares to skin a caribou he has just shot while hunting on Baffin Island. Above: a hunter's wife removes a ringed seal's skin from a drying frame at her home in Savissivik and (overleaf) a female polar bear and her cubs make their way across the sea ice of Hudson Bay.

Spring

Facing page top: an adult harp seal nursing her pup on an ice floe. The richness of the mother's milk enables the pups, which weigh, on average, fifteen pounds at birth, to gain fifty pounds by the time they are weaned, twelve to fourteen days later. A pup (top) will lose its white coat completely by the time it is a month old. The Arctic tern (above) flies over 12,000 miles, the longest migration of any bird, to breed in the high Arctic each summer. Facing page bottom: an Arctic fox. Overleaf: Iqaluit (formerly Frobisher Bay), on Baffin Island, the administrative centre of Canada's Eastern Arctic.

In these scenes from Inuit life, Navarana (top) has her hair combed by Inaluk in a hunters hut at Narssaarssuk, Saufak Kiviok (above) adjusts the flame of a Primus stove, two boys (facing page bottom) play a traditional 'trial of strength' game in Siorapaluk, and Ere and Bergithe Danielsen (facing page top) pose for the photographer in their home at Moriussaq.

Top: two Inuit hunters pause to listen for walruses while hunting on newly-formed sea ice, and (above left) Peter Peary hurls his harpoon at a walrus that has just surfaced at a breathing hole in the ice and hauls the dead creature (above right) to the surface. Facing page: (top) hunters preparing to attach a rope to a dead walrus, and (bottom) huskies being used to haul the carcase, weighing over a ton, onto the sea ice.

Top: using a white linen screen mounted on small skis to conceal himself, Kauguanak Kissuk stalks a seal basking on the sea ice, and (above) with harpoon at the ready, Peter Peary carefully approaches a walrus that has just surfaced at a breathing hole. Facing page: (top) walruses surface in a lead in the sea ice, and (bottom) Inuit hunters from Cape Dorset, Baffin Island, hunt seals from an ice floe. Overleaf: a group of hunters in Melville Bay silhouetted against the sunlight and frost smoke rising off the open water at -30°C.

EVINRUDE

Top: Inuit hunters prepare for a dog sled race on Armed Forces Day at Thule Air Base in Greenland, while (above) two hunters take their ease on the sea ice. Facing page: (bottom) Mamarut Kristiansen rests in his tent after a day's hunting and (top) Inuit families shop at the Hudson Bay Company's store at Igloolik. Overleaf: a herd of walruses in pack ice near Etah.

Hudson's Bay Company
the Bay FOODS
ski-doo
5500
POLARIS

Puppies behave in very much the same way, feeding from their mother (top) and snuggling up to her for warmth and security (above and facing page), all over the world, whether by the warmth of a fireside or, as here, in the frozen reaches of the far north.

Top left: an Inuit girl plays with a puppy at a spring hunting camp. Top right: Kaviganguak wipes his brow after the exertion of dragging a dead seal across the ice. Above: Arctic fox and seal skins in the trading store at Moriussaq. Facing page: a portrait of Inaluk and (overleaf) a cloud of *dovkies* (little auks). Millions of these small, squat sea birds arrive in Northwest Greenland each spring to breed.

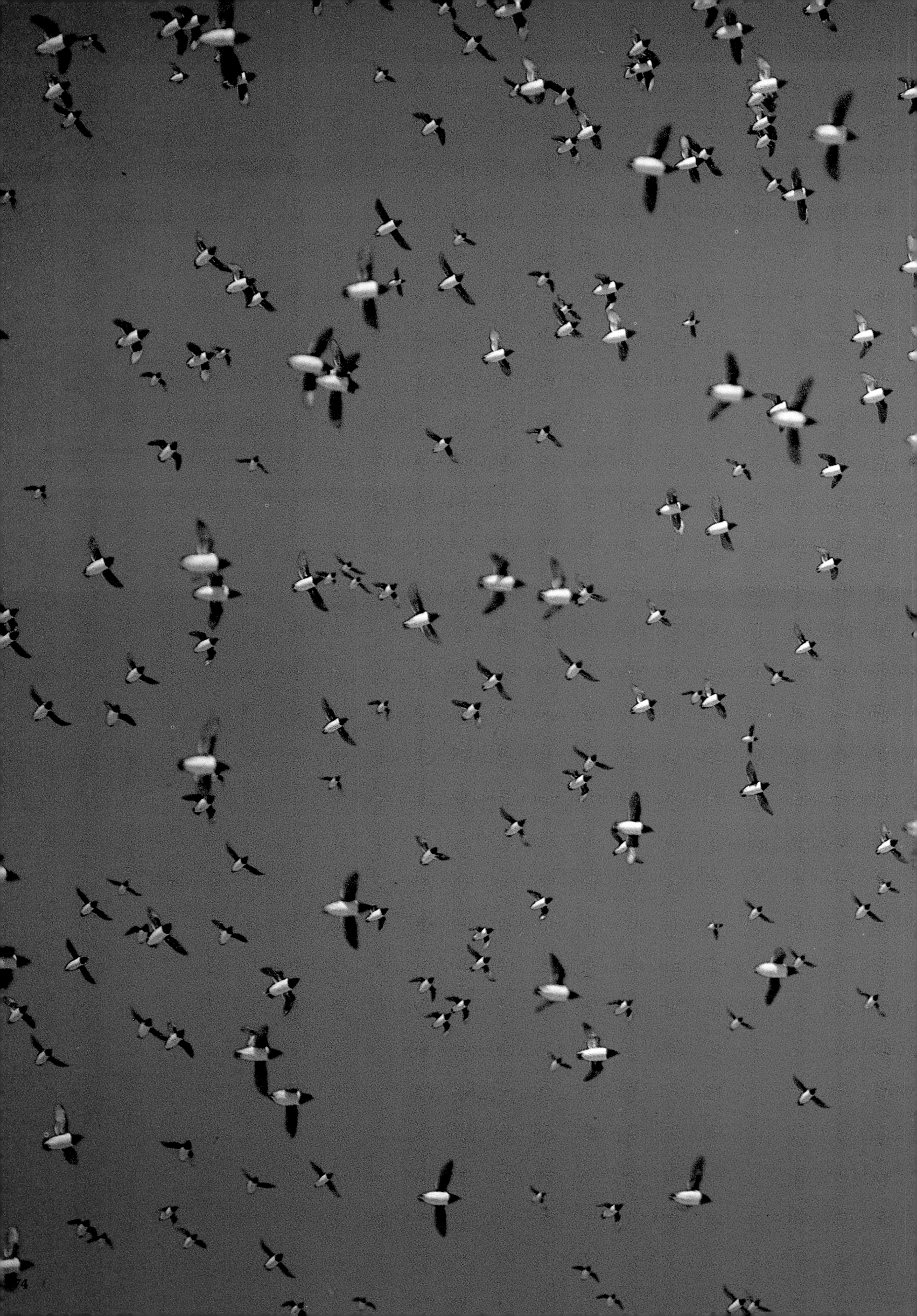

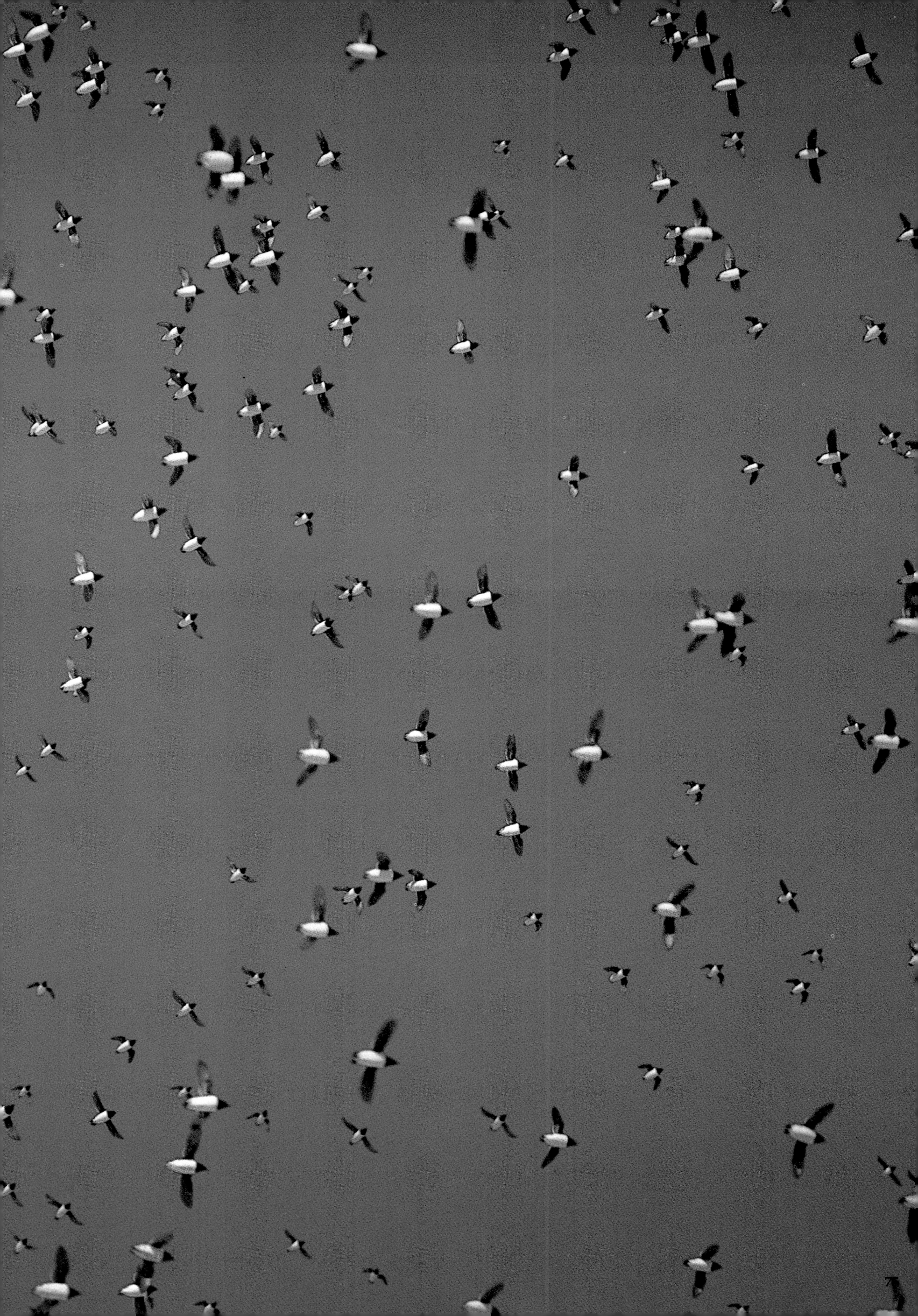

Facing page: a young gyrfalcon and (top) a herd of musk-oxen in East Greenland. The latters remarkably thick coats provide ideal protection against the High Arctic's bitter cold. Above: an Arctic fox and (overleaf) a harp seal surfacing by an ice floe to check on her young pup.

An Inuit hunter (top left) examines a guillemot he has just shot, and (left) a harpooned narwhal is butchered at the ice edge. Top: Alekasinguak chews a piece of bearded seal skin to soften it sufficently for it be used for the sole of traditional Inuit boots known as 'kamik.' Above: a polar bear skin stretched out on a frame to dry in the spring sunshine. Facing page: Kigutikak Dunek drinks from a melt pool on the sea ice. During the spring the salt in the sea ice sinks, leaving the upper level relatively salt-free and drinkable. Overleaf: Karkutsiak Kristiansen out seal hunting in his boat near Moriussaq.

Above: the crystal-like beauty of meltwater plunging over a rock cliff face on Saunders Island. Facing page top: Hans Kristiansen manoeuvres his boat between ice floes at the mouth of Granville Fjord, where (overleaf) a massive iceberg is bathed in soft light from the midnight sun. Facing page bottom: a hunter jumps a lead in the sea ice ahead of his dog team (photograph © 1981 Time-Life Books B.V. from the *Peoples of the Wild* series).

Top: Jakob Petersen ties improvised boots onto one of his huskies to protect its feet from being lacerated by sharp crystals on the summer ice, and (above) Saufak Kiviok hangs up a sealskin to dry. Facing page: (bottom) Nukapainguak uses a throwing board to launch his kayak harpoon (photographs © 1981 Time-Life Books B.V. from the *Peoples of the Wild* series), and (top) Karkutsiak Kristiansen shoots at a seal from his boat while out hunting near Moriussaq. Overleaf: a large iceberg floats amidst a mass of broken ice in Inglefield Sound.

Facing page: (bottom) icebergs and sea ice after break-up in Inglefield Sound, and (top) Kulutenguak, after a successful hunting trip, paddling his sealskin-covered kayak back to camp. Above: netting dovkies.

Top: perfectly balanced in his kayak, Nukapainguak prepares to throw a harpoon while out hunting in Inglefield Sound, and (above) Jakob Petersen fishes for sea sculpin through a hole in the sea ice. Facing page: icicles formed on a huge block of sea ice during the frost of a summer's night. Overleaf: his frail kayak dwarfed by a massive iceberg, Kulutenguak hunts for seals amongst the broken ice in Inglefield Sound (photograph © 1981 Time-Life Books B.V. from the *Peoples of the Wild* series).

Above: Eqilat carrying her young son in a sealskin *amaut* (hooded jacket), (facing page top) Inuit women at Qeqertat sewing a sealskin cover onto a kayak frame, and (facing page bottom) Moriussaq Inuit Settlement.

Top: Ituku and (overleaf) two Inuit hunters paddle their kayaks between ice floes in Inglefield Sound, while (facing page top) an Inuit boy fishes for sea sculpin off an ice floe at Qeqertat, and other youngsters play 'rock the floe' by running from one side to the other. Facing page bottom: an Inuit summer camp on the north side of Inglefield Sound and (above) Inuit hunters arriving by boat at a summer camp near Qeqertat.

Top: Kulutenguak returns to camp at high tide and (above) hunters prepare to go out in their kayaks from a narwhal hunting camp at Kikertarrugguak. Facing page: silhouetted by the midnight sun, a hunter paddles his kayak in Inglefield Sound, and (overleaf) Ituku pursues a pod of narwhals in Academy Bay.

Top: Inuit hunters butcher a narwhal at Qeqertat and (above) Mikile Kristiansen flenses a male narwhal on the shore at Qingmiuneqarfik. Facing page: the waters are stained deep red as a narwhal is butchered. Overleaf: a hunter in his kayak among the giant icebergs of Inglefield Sound.

Facing page bottom: Mesauna Kristiansen chases a pod of narwhals, (below) Uusaqqak Henson cleans a freshly-caught sea trout in MacCormick Fjord and, on a sunny July day, Ituku (facing page top) navigates his boat between ice floes near Moriussaq. Bottom: hunters return to their boat moored near Josephine Peary Island. Overleaf: low tide reveals the sculptural form of a grounded iceberg.

Flowers of the north. Top left: broad-leaved willow herb, Greenland's national flower, (top right) mountain avens, (above) Arctic poppies and (facing page) three-toothed saxifrage.

Above: sharp against a deep blue sky, kittiwakes fly above the bird cliffs on Saunders Island, where dawn colours the sky and sea (overleaf). Facing page: (top) a summer storm gathers over Inglefield Sound and (bottom) a large iceberg looms at the mouth of Granville Fjord.

Backlit by the low October sun, a polar bear (facing page) roams the shore of Hudson Bay and a young gull (top) stands on newly formed sea ice, while (overleaf) a hunter makes use of the few hours of sunlight during an October day to hunt seals among drifting icebergs. Above: a grounded iceberg at sunset.

Facing page: (top) a polar bear nurses her cubs of the year and (bottom) Jens Danielsen steers his boat through the thickening sea ice while out hunting seals near Saunders Island. Above: a contemplative portrait of Ittok Danielsen.

Facing page top: hunters returning to Moriussaq, and (above) Sofie Jensen from Qaanaaq warmly wrapped in fox skin clothing. Facing page bottom: icebergs drifting in a calm sea off Saunders Island, and (overleaf) a massive iceberg bathed in the golden light of an early October day.

Ituku preparing to harpoon a bearded seal from his boat (top), skinning a ringed seal (above) caught in one of his nets, and feeding sealmeat to his huskies (facing page bottom) outside his home in Moriussaq. Facing page top: icebergs on the horizon in the pink light of dawn, and (overleaf) a hunter out seal hunting in his boat.

Above: huskies curl up for shelter against an October storm at Moriussaq, where (top) a sealskin hangs up to dry alongside the family's washing on a line outside a hunter's home. Facing page: hunters struggle to navigate their boat through a narrow channel in the thickening sea ice.

Facing page: Ituku prepares to shoot at a seal, (top) Jens and Tukaq returning from a seal hunt. and (above) a Bell Jetranger lands at Moriussaq. Helicopters act as a lifeline to the remote settlements of North Greenland. Overleaf: Itudlak Danielsen returns to Moriussaq after a seal hunting trip in the fall.

WITH 400

Above: Baker Lake settlement in the Keewatin district of Northern Canada. Top: Inuit children guide the sled as a hunter leads his dog team down onto the sea ice. Facing page: Tukaq Kristiansen. Overleaf: after leaving his boat, Avataq Henson cautiously picks his way across the thin ice of Moriussaq's natural harbour.

Facing page: (top) Arctic hares, the skins of which will be used to make the inner sock for *kamik* (boots), hang outside a house at Moriussaq and (bottom) sealskins hang on a hunter's meat rack. Below: a dog sled travelling across new ice in October, and (bottom) huskies at feeding time. Overleaf: icebergs and October's low sun create a dramatic backdrop as a hunter attends to his boat.

At Baker Lake, an Inuit family watches television in their home (facing page top), and an Inuit disc jockey (top left) works at the local radio station, while at Moriussaq, hunters (above centre left) clean a pair of walrus tusks. After the arrival of a helicopter at Moriussaq, where Ilaituk (above) teaches at the school, Inuit children (facing page bottom) rush the mail bag to the store by sled. Top right: Massautsiak Eipe drum singing, a traditional Inuit pastime, at his home in Qaanaaq. Overleaf: the mid-October sun sets over the freezing sea.

Above: close to an iceberg, Jens Danielsen sets a net under the sea ice to catch seals while, in high spirits during a hunting trip, Mamarut Kristiansen performs a handstand (facing page top) on the sea ice. Facing page bottom: after spending the night in an igloo, a group of Inuit from Baker Lake prepare to continue their caribou hunt. Overleaf: thickening sea ice, as winter approaches in Inglefield Sound, reflected in the pink light of an October sun.

YAMAHA

Top: hunting in November by the light of the full moon, Ituku checks a seal's breathing hole in the sea ice. Above: icebergs at the mouth of Granville Fjord, sidelit by the low autumn sun. To encourage his huskies to hunt polar bears (overleaf), Ituku (facing page) drapes himself in a bearskin before approaching them, growling and feigning attack.